Arguably the most famous lighthouse of all is the Eddystone, which marks a rock formation fourteen miles off Plymouth that is a major hazard to shipping. The current tower is the fourth major structure built on the rocks since 1698. Other lighthouses on the South Devon coast have been built at Berry Head and Start Point, while Bull Point and Lynmouth Foreland on the North Devon coast guide shipping up the Bristol Channel.

However, aids to navigation alone were not enough and concern about ship losses expressed at the end of the eighteenth century led to the development of some form of boat on shore ready to put out to save vessels in distress. Before lifeboats were operated, rescues were performed by local people often using their own boats, but by the early 1800s the first lifeboats were being built. The first lifeboats in Devon were either operated from or funded by populations in the larger towns, notably Exmouth (funded from Exeter), Plymouth and Appledore (with influences from Bideford).

But there was no co-ordination of lifeboat stations or lifeboat building on a national basis until the 1820s, when the RNLI was founded as a result of the exertions of Sir William Hillary, of Douglas in the Isle of Man. At a meeting in London on 4 March 1824, the Royal National Institution for thePreservation of Life from Shipwreck (RNIPLS) came into being, with its sole responsibility as the preservation of human life from shipwreck.

The organisation was known as the RNIPLS until being renamed and reformed during the 1850s. Since then it has gone from strength to strength, building new lifeboats, establishing new lifeboat stations and developing ever more sophisticated lifeboat designs. The first motor lifeboats in the early twentieth century were followed by inshore lifeboats in the 1960s, and ever more powerful and advanced self-righting lifeboats at the end of the century.

The sailing ships and merchant craft were the lifeboat service's main customers during the nineteenth century, but today the plethora of pleasure craft and fun seekers are the ones most in need of lifeboat assistance. Incidents to which rescue craft are called are now numerous, and during 2008 the RNLI's thirty-five lifeboat stations in the south-west, including those in Cornwall, launched 1,567 times, rescuing 1,671 people and spending more than 2,150 hours at sea on emergency call outs. Today, five lifeboats operating from three stations on the North Devon coast, and nine from five stations on the South Devon coast, cover the sea areas off the county's coast.

SIDMOUTH

Sidmouth lifeboat station was established by the RNLI in 1869 primarily as an intermediate station between Exmouth to the west, and Lyme Regis, in Dorset, to the east, providing protection for the coastal traffic using Lyme Bay. Two self-righting lifeboats, both built by Woolfe at Shadwell in London, served the station during its forty-three year existence and are credited with saving a total of thirty-eight lives. The first, named *Rimington*, was on station from 1860 to 1885, and the second, *William and Frances*, from May 1885 to 1912.

Sidmouth lifeboat crew circa 1900 wearing their cork life-jackets.

A lifeboat house, now no longer in existence, was built on the corner of Ham Lane on a site which is now marked by a plaque over a doorway. The station's closure in September 1912 came about because of the decline of the coastal trade, as demonstrated by the fact that, after 1883, only one effective service was performed. A lifeboat was not needed at Sidmouth, and could not be justified by the RNLI.

More than half-a-century later, a lifeboat was again operated from Sidmouth, although not under the auspices of the RNLI. In the mid-1960s leisure activities were increasing in the area, and in 1968 students from the local secondary school formed a surf life-saving organisation, which initially maintained beach patrols during the weekends in summer. The organisation subsequently became the Sidmouth Lifeboat Service.

The service gradually acquired more

Recovering the 34ft self-righter *William and Frances*, which was on station from 1885 to 1912.

The plaque over the doorway of the building on the site of the original boathouse. NICHOLAS LEACH

The independent inshore lifeboat *Sidmouth Herald* outside the boathouse on Sidmouth seafront. NICHOLAS LEACH

capable rescue equipment, starting in 1972 when cover was significantly improved with the purchase of a 16ft Atlantic rigid-inflatable, fitted with a 40hp outboard engine, for daytime patrols and surf rescue. Operational hours were gradually extended throughout the 1970s until, with the purchase of a pager system, 24-hour cover was possible. In 1982 Sidmouth Inshore Rescue Service became a declared rescue facility with the Coastguard and was available for callouts all day every day.

Bigger and better lifeboats were purchased, and in 1991 *Spirit of Sidmouth*, a 5m Humber type boat, was acquired. In April 1998 an Atlantic 21 was bought from the RNLI after it had ended its service life with the Institution. To house the new lifeboat, which was named *Sidmouth Herald*, a new boathouse was needed

along with a new launching system, which included a specially-modified Renault tractor and launching trailer.

Sidmouth Herald was replaced in October 2004 by a larger and faster rigid-inflatable, the Arctic 24 type *Pride of Sidmouth*. She was built by VT Halmatic and funded through the efforts of local people with the backing of the *Sunday Mercury* newspaper in Birmingham. Powered by twin 135hp outboard motors, she carries four crew, has a top speed of over forty knots and is larger, heavier and faster than any of the previous lifeboats. The lifeboat covers an area from Beer Head in the east to Otterton Ledge in the west.

Recovery of *Sidmouth Herald*, the Atlantic 21 inshore lifeboat purchased from the RNLI and in service with the independent service until 2004. NICHOLAS LEACH

The lifeboat house built in 1903 and used for the offshore lifeboat and then the inshore lifeboat, doubling up as a souvenir outlet and display centre. NICHOLAS LEACH

Catherine Harriott Eaton, a 35ft 6in motor self-righter, was the first motor lifeboat to serve at Exmouth.

EXMOUTH

The first lifeboat at Exmouth was a North Country type boat built by Henry Greathead at South Shields in 1803. She was funded by local subscriptions and a £50 contribution from the Corporation of Lloyds. A boathouse was built near Passage House, but this was washed away during a storm in 1814 and the station lapsed until reopened by the RNLI in the second half of the nineteenth century.

The placing of a lifeboat at Exmouth by the RNLI in 1858 was largely due to the efforts of Lieut J. D. Agassiz, who became the station's first Honorary Secretary, and Lady Rolle, of Bicton, who provided the

funds necessary for the establishment of the station. A lifeboat house was built on the beach in 1859, on a site leased by the Hon Mark Rolle, after a small 30ft six-oared self-righting lifeboat was supplied to the station towards the end of 1858. This first lifeboat, named *Victoria* at the suggestion of her donor, served for nine years but was not instrumental in saving any lives.

The next lifeboat, funded by Lady Rolle and also named *Victoria*, was another self-righter, and served for seven years before being replaced in 1884 by yet another self-righter. This next boat, 34ft and ten-oared, was funded by Mrs J. Somes, of Annery House near Bideford, and named *Joseph*

The motor lifeboat *Catherine Harriott Eaton* setting out on exercise.

Somes, the first of two boats so named which served Exmouth for almost the next fifty years. The first *Joseph Somes* launched eleven times on services, rescuing three from the cutter *Topsy*, of Torquay, in October 1889, and four from the ketch *Mater Dei* in December 1891.

The second *Joseph Somes*, a 35ft self-righter, arrived in November 1903 at which point the old house of 1859 was deemed too small for the new craft so it was then demolished, and a new lifeboat house was built on the same site. *Joseph Somes*, which proved to be the station's last pulling lifeboat, only completed ten effective services in her thirty years on station, but when the time came to replace her, in the 1930s, the station was upgraded while others closed down as the RNLI took into account the greater capabilities of the motor lifeboat.

The station's first motor lifeboat, a 35ft 6in self-righter named *Catherine Harriet Eaton*, arrived in August 1933. A motor tractor was also provided to speed up the launch procedure. *Catherine Harriet Eaton* served for twenty years and saved thirty-one lives, before being replaced in October 1953 by a 35ft 6in Liverpool motor named *Maria Noble*. She was the last carriage-launched lifeboat at Exmouth for almost half a century, and completed

The 46ft Watson motor lifeboat *Michael Stephens*, which served from 1963 to 1968 and saved eleven lives, approaching Exmouth Docks.

thirty service launches in her eight years on station.

In 1961, the station was supplied with a larger lifeboat, the 45ft 6in Watson motor *George and Sarah Strachan*, which was kept afloat at moorings in the estuary off Exmouth Docks. A wooden boarding boat, launched by davit from the east pier of the dock entrance, was supplied for the crew to reach her and crew facilities were provided on the quayside. Two further Watson motor lifeboats were on station during the 1960s, as the larger lifeboats were seen as better able to cope with severe local conditions on the river bar, as

The 48ft 6in Solent *City of Birmingham* after her naming ceremony on 16 May 1970. Jeff Morris

7

No.89 (later D-89), the first inshore lifeboat to serve at Exmouth. JEFF MORRIS

44ft Waveney *Louis Marchesi of Round Table*, which was on station for two years, leaves Exmouth Dock. NICHOLAS LEACH

well as having a greater range in case of calls on the far side of Lyme Bay.

Meanwhile, the 1903 boathouse, used by the lifeboat until 1961, was converted into a Lifeboat Display Centre, and was later converted to house the inshore lifeboats, the first of which was sent to the station in May 1966. The ILB soon proved its worth when, on 29 May 1966, it was used to save three bathers who were in difficulty in heavy seas two miles south west of Exmouth. The Thanks on Vellum were accorded to Coxswain Brian Rowsell and crew member Peter Rowsell for their efforts during this service.

In 1970, a new lifeboat, funded by the City of Birmingham Lifeboat Appeal, was sent to the station. Named *City of Birmingham*, she was a 48ft 6in Solent type, steel-hulled, self-righting, and powered by twin 110hp Gardner engines. In just over thirteen years at Exmouth, she carried out fifty-eight services, but by the 1980s was deemed too slow. She was therefore replaced in August 1983 by a faster lifeboat, named *Caroline Finch*, which was one of only twelve 33ft Brede class lifeboats to be built.

During her eleven years on station, *Caroline Finch* launched 178 times on service and saved sixty-four lives making her by far the busiest Exmouth lifeboat hitherto. She was involved in a notable rescue on 7 April 1985 when she went to a sunken speedboat. As the lifeboat crossed the bar, very heavy seas were encountered but, once at sea, the lifeboat crew spotted the three people in the water. It was too dangerous to get close enough to them to be able to lift them out, so lifeboatman Geoffrey Ingram entered the water to assist the casualties. He supported the two girls, while the man swam to the lifeboat. All were pulled on board and landed at Exmouth, suffering from shock and hypothermia. The Thanks on Vellum was accorded to Ingram in recognition of his actions.

By the 1990s, the RNLI was looking to phase out the Bredes, and in 1994 *Caroline Finch* was replaced by the 1977-built *Louis Marchesi of Round Table*, a 44ft Waveney which had spent most of her career at Newhaven. She served until July 1996, when she was replaced by another lifeboat funded by an appeal in the City of Birmingham.

The IB1 type inshore lifeboat *George Bearman* (D-669) launching at the end of her naming ceremony. PAUL RICHARDS

14m Trent *Forward Birmingham* arriving on station in 1996. She served the station until May 2008. NICHOLAS LEACH

Relief 14m Trent *Dora Foster McDougall* on exercise off Exmouth in 2007.
NICHOLAS LEACH

The new lifeboat, named *Forward Birmingham*, was a 14m Trent, one of the RNLI's latest design of all-weather lifeboat with a speed of twenty-five knots. She was kept afloat, like her immediate predecessors, off Exmouth Dock, and boarded by her crew via an inflatable boarding boat. However, despite her considerable capabilities, *Forward Birmingham* was hampered by problems with the silting of the river Exe, particularly at the river entrance, which meant that she was often operating only on restricted service.

Various efforts were made to overcome the launching limitations until, in 2006, a decision was made that the station would revert to a carriage launch and a new lifeboat house would be built. Launching trials using a 12m Mersey, tractor and carriage were undertaken, and in 2007 plans for the new house were submitted. In May 2008, before the house was completed, *Forward Birmingham* was replaced by 12m Mersey *Margaret Jean*, which had a shallower draft and could cross the bar more safely and easily.

In 2008-9 a new all-purpose house was built near Maer Rocks. The new building housed both the D class ILB and the 12m Mersey lifeboat, which was launched down a ramp and onto the beach. It provided considerably enhanced training and shore facilities for the crew. *Margaret Jean*, the tenth motor lifeboat to serve at Exmouth, was kept at moorings while the new house was constructed, but was recovered onto her carriage for the first time in summer 2009 and a new chapter in the station's history began.

14m Trent *Forward Birmingham* and 12m Mersey *Margaret Jean* at moorings during the changeover from the former to the latter.
PETER EDEY

9

The lifeboat house built in 1863 on The Den, with the second *China* lifeboat (on station 1864 to 1880) outside. By courtesy of the RNLI

TEIGNMOUTH

Teignmouth's first lifeboat was provided by the Shipwrecked Fishermen and Mariners' Royal Benevolent Society (SFMRBS), which was founded in February 1839. The Society's main aim was to help people who had been shipwrecked and, for an annual subscription, would give assistance to the dependants of its members who had lost their lives at sea. However, it also established a number of lifeboat stations and funded several lifeboats during the 1850s, including that at Teignmouth. This first lifeboat, a 28ft self-righting type built and designed by James Beeching, was kept in an existing boathouse on the beach, near the Custom House.

Between 1851 and October 1854, the SFMRBS formally handed over control of the stations it established to the RNLI, and so the lifeboats at Lytham, Rhyl, Portmadoc, Tenby, Llanelli, Hornsea and Newhaven, as well as that of Teignmouth, came under the auspices of the national institution. The RNLI formally took over the Teignmouth station in 1854, and the boathouse on the beach continued in use until 1862 when a new and larger house was built on The Den, with doors facing the harbour to make launching easier and faster.

Soon after the new boathouse had been completed, Teignmouth was supplied with an experimental iron lifeboat for trials. The boat, named *China*, was a 33ft self-righter designed by Joseph Prowse, the RNLI's Surveyor, and fitted with ten oars. She arrived in October 1863 but was replaced less than a year later, and was not deemed a success. The new

The second *Alfred Staniforth* lifeboat is capsized as part of a lifeboat day demonstration, watched by hundreds of people. From an old postcard supplied by Graham Brailey

lifeboat was also named *China*, a standard wooden-hulled 32ft self-righter, and was also funded by the staff of Gilman & Sons in their Hong Kong and Shanghai offices.

The second *China* was renamed *Arnold* in 1880, and this lifeboat went on to serve until 1887, saving almost fifty lives in twenty-three years on station. The next new lifeboat on station was also named *Arnold*, both boats being appropriated to the fund of the Devon and Cornwall Lifeboat Bazaar. The second *Arnold*, a 34ft self-righter, served until 1896 when she was replaced by a slightly larger lifeboat, named *Alfred Staniforth*, which served for more than thirty years during which time she saved sixty-four lives.

The most outstanding rescue in the history of the station took place on 10 October 1907, after the schooner *Tehwija* of Riga, got into difficulty in a strong south-westerly gale and very heavy sea, and ran aground on the outer part of the Pole Sands. *Alfred Staniforth* was launched into the difficult conditions but, as she was crossing the bar in exceptionally rough seas, a heavy sea caught her, knocked down every crewman and washed the oars overboard.

The oars were held in their lanyards

(Denney & Co.) TEIGNMOUTH LIFEBOAT DAY, September 8th, 1904.

Watched by a large crowd, on lifeboat day in September 1904, the second *Alfred Staniforth* lifeboat is launched from her carriage. FROM AN OLD POSTCARD SUPPLIED BY GRAHAM BRAILEY

and so the crew recovered them, regained control of their boat and a fresh start was made. This time the bar was safely crossed and the lifeboat reached the open sea. The crew of *Tehwija* were in the rigging as waves broke over their vessel. The lifeboat's anchor was dropped and she veered down on the casualty to establish communication, achieved with great difficulty. The eight crew were then rescued by ropes, while the schooner became a complete wreck within fifteen minutes of the rescue being completed. For this rescue, Silver medals were awarded to W. J. Burden, the Honorary Secretary, who steered the lifeboat to enable the Coxswain and Bowman to assist in double banking the oars, and to Coxswain George Rice.

The last pulling lifeboat at Teignmouth was a 35ft self-righter named *Henry Finlay*, built in 1911 for the Macrihanish station in Scotland, which arrived in April 1930. She remained at Teignmouth for a decade, launching only three times and saving one life. By 1940, the motor lifeboat had taken over and the seas off Teignmouth were deemed to be adequately covered by the motor lifeboats at Exmouth and Brixham and the station was temporarily closed on 6 November 1940. However, *Henry Finlay* was left in the boathouse on standby until the station was permanently closed in July 1945 when the boat was sold into private ownership.

The lifeboat house of 1863 was in private ownership after the station closed until being re-acquired when the RNLI reopened the station with the Atlantic inshore lifeboats.
NICHOLAS LEACH

The scene outside the boathouse during the naming of the Atlantic 85 *The Two Annes* (B-809) on 4 August 2006. NICHOLAS LEACH

Following the closure of the station in 1940, the lifeboat remained in the boathouse until it was sold in 1945; the house was then used as a café, but was then neglected for a number of years. In March 1990, the station was reopened by the RNLI for evaluation trials as an inshore lifeboat station. A temporary Atlantic 21, B-538 *Lord Brotherton*, was declared operational on 3 November following a period of intensive crew training, but was replaced two weeks later by another relief Atlantic 21, B-533, which stayed for a year.

Launch of *The Two Annes* at the end of her naming ceremony, watched by crowds of well-wishers. NICHOLAS LEACH

Meanwhile, the 1863 lifeboat house was re-acquired in 1991 and extensively renovated and converted to accommodate the Atlantic 21 and its launching rig. A year after the station had been reopened, a new Atlantic 21, B-588 *Frank and Dorothy*, was supplied and placed on station on 11 December 1991. Funded from the bequest of Mrs Dorothy Maud North, this lifeboat served at Teignmouth for almost fifteen years and provided outstanding service. When replaced in 2006, she was one of the last remaining Atlantic 21 ILBs on station. The new boat, B-809, a larger and more powerful Atlantic 85, was declared operational on 1 August 2006 and christened *The Two Annes* at a ceremony on 4 August 2006 by the donor, Anne Bache, after herself and her sister-in-law, Ann.

The crew of the Atlantic 85 *The Two Annes* acknowledge the crowds at the end of her naming ceremony. NICHOLAS LEACH

TORQUAY

Torquay, now one of England's premier holiday resorts, had a lifeboat station for just under half a century from the 1870s to the 1920s. At a public meeting held in September 1875, local people petitioned the RNLI to form a lifeboat station as the coastal traffic of the time meant a station between Brixham and Teignmouth was needed. A lifeboat house was built in 1875 at the Ladies Bathing Cove, the only practical site, and this was used throughout the life of the station. It later became a café until being demolished in September 1975.

The lifeboat house built in 1876 in the Ladies Bathing Cove and used until the station closed in 1923.

The first lifeboat was a standard self-righting craft, 33ft in length, pulling ten oars and carriage launched. She was named *Mary Brundrett* and served for thirteen years, saving nineteen lives. On 14 October 1881 she capsized with thirteen crew on board when returning from service. She was caught out in a squall in the middle of Torbay, but she righted herself and all the crew were fortunately able to scramble back on board with no loss of life.

The second lifeboat was another self-righter, the 37ft twelve-oared *James and Eliza Woodall*, built by Watkins at Blackwall, and fitted with sliding keels and water ballast tanks. She was a fine sailing lifeboat, but during her thirteen years on station never undertook a life-saving service. She was replaced in April 1902 by a 38ft Watson type sailing lifeboat, which widened the scope of the station as the design was intended as a sailing craft. Named *Wighton*, the new lifeboat remained on station for just over two decades. In 1922, launching the boat across the beach became more difficult and this, together with the arrival the previous year of a motor lifeboat at Brixham, resulted in the closure of the station on 31 March 1923.

Between 1917 and 1928, Mr W. Ball, jnr, of the Whiteways & Ball shipowning firm, presented to the RNLI a 20ft 9in ship's lifeboat to be called the Torquay Harbour Lifesaving Boat. The boat was given on the understanding that it would remain at Torquay even if the lifeboat station was closed, and it was suggested she might be used for rescue work during the summer months. She was initially kept on davits on Beacon Quay, later moored afloat, and was in the end used only for rescue work in the harbour. One rescue only is recorded as being performed by the Lifesaving Boat, on 7 January 1919 to the Hull schooner *Skell*, which was assisted to safety.

The self-righting lifeboat *James and Eliza Woodall* with her crew outside the lifeboat house.

The 37ft self-righter *Betsy Newbon*, the last pulling and sailing lifeboat at Brixham, was on station from 1896 to 1922. BY COURTESY OF RNLI

TORBAY

The lifeboat station which covers Torbay has always been operated from Brixham, and although the station is now known as Torbay, it was originally named Brixham. Between 1917 and 1924 it was known as Brixham & Paignton, but since 1924 the station has been titled Torbay to reflect the sea area covered.

The station was established following a storm in January 1866 in which more than forty vessels were wrecked in Torbay and many lives were lost. The RNLI immediately took steps to remedy the situation, and in October 1866 a new lifeboat, the 34ft self-righter *City of Exeter*, was sent to the station. A lifeboat house

The first motor lifeboat at Torbay, *Alfred and Clara Heath*, was also the first motor lifeboat in South Devon. She served from 1922 to 1930 and then operated from Salcombe until 1938.

was constructed at Bolton Cross in Brixham from where the lifeboat could be take on its carriage down Fore Street for launching in the harbour or along the coast to other places more convenient for launching. This house was used until 1873 and has since been demolished.

In 1873 a new lifeboat house was built near the corner of the breakwater at Brixham harbour, with a slipway for a launch into the harbour. It housed the first lifeboat, which launched five times and saved just one life, until 1885. Between 1885 and 1894 a larger 37ft self-righter named *Brian Bates* was on station, and she was replaced by a 38ft twelve-oared self-righter. This boat, *Betsey Newbon*, was found to be too large and so another 37ft self-righter, also named *Betsey Newbon*, was sent Brixham two years later. The second *Betsey Newbon*, which was also the last pulling and sailing lifeboat at the station, served for twenty-six years and enjoyed a distinguished career, saving forty-six lives.

At the end of the First World War the RNLI began to build motor lifeboats, and a new motor craft was allocated to the station. The new motor lifeboat, the first of five 40ft motor self-righters built by J. S. White at Cowes in 1921-2, arrived in March 1922. Named *Alfred and Clara Heath*, she was fitted with a single 45hp petrol engine and also carried oars and sail in case the engine failed. She was the first motor lifeboat in South Devon and, after just over eight years at Torbay, was transferred to Salcombe.

In the 1920s motor lifeboat development continued apace and a large 51ft Barnett motor type was developed which, with twin engines, had a long range and was suited for deep-sea work being fitted with a cabin for ten persons. One of the new type was sent to Torbay. The new lifeboat, named *George Shee* after a Secretary of the RNLI, greatly improved the capabilities of the station and enabled a greater area to be covered.

The lifeboat was placed on moorings in the harbour in 1930, close to the lifeboat house, and a boarding boat was supplied. The house was retained for use as a crew facility but during the Second World War the slipway was buried under a concrete apron built for amphibious craft, and the house itself was halved in length.

Between 1935 and 1939, Torbay lifeboat and her crew were involved in four outstanding rescues which resulted in Coxswain William Mogridge being awarded two Bronze and two Silver medals for gallantry. The first of these services, on 30 December 1935, was to the trawler *Satanicle*, which was in distress fifteen miles east of Start Point in a south-westerly gale and heavy seas. Three crew members from *Satanicle* had been rescued by another vessel, and with great difficulty the last member of the crew, the skipper, was saved by the lifeboat.

In 1937 Mogridge was awarded a clasp to the Bronze Medal for the service

to the steamer *English Trader* which ran ashore on Checkstone Ledge at the entrance to Dartmouth Harbour on 23 January. The lifeboat had stood by all night in gale force winds. Heavy seas, with waves 15ft high, were breaking over the steamer which was being pounded on the rocks and was about to break up when the lifeboat saved the fifty-two men on board in an extremely hazardous operation.

The Silver medal-winning rescues came in 1938 and 1939. The first was on 9 December 1938, when two people in the open motor crabber *Channel Pride* were rescued after their vessel was caught by a sudden gale off Coombe Point, Dartmouth. Just over a year later, on 16 December 1939, a clasp to the Silver Medal was awarded to Coxswain Mogridge and Bronze Medals went to three other members of the crew for the rescue of seven persons from the schooner *Henrietta*, of Truro, which had been carried by strong tides and a north-easterly gale to the edge of a dangerous reef south of Dartmouth.

During the war years, particularly 1944, *George Shee* was particularly busy, and on 17 December that year another outstanding medal-winning rescue was carried out. The lifeboat saved nineteen men from the tug *Empire Alfred* and Yard Craft No.345, which the tug was towing, which had both gone ashore at Hollicombe in a south-easterly gale. Getting alongside each vessel to effect the rescue proved to be very difficult in shallow water. Coxswain Frederick Sanders

George Shee at moorings in Brixham Outer Harbour. BY COURTESY OF GRAHAME FARR

Princess Alexandra of Kent at moorings in the harbour with the inshore lifeboat A-2, a 20ft 6in Hatch type boat built in 1967. BY COURTESY OF GRAHAME FARR

awarded the Silver medal and the Bronze Second-Service Clasp went to Mechanic Richard Harris.

In July 1958 a new lifeboat was sent to the station and *George Shee*, after saving almost 200 lives in twenty-eight years of service, was retired. The new boat was a 52ft Barnett, larger and more powerful than her predecessor, and built at a cost of £38,500. She was named *Princess Alexander of Kent* and served at Torbay for seventeen years, saving sixty-nine lives and launching 157 times on service.

During her first full year of service at Torbay, *Princess Alexander of Kent* was involved in an outstanding rescue. On 7

December 1959 she put out after the Dutch tug *Cycloop*, which was sheltering with three lighters in tow, requested help. The master had cut one lighter adrift leaving two men stranded on it. In gale force winds and rough seas, Coxswain Henry Thomas and his crew found the lighter aground so the lifeboat was anchored and veered towards it. Heavy seas were sweeping it, and at times the lifeboat was lifted above the level of the lighter's deck. Coxswain Thomas managed to bring the lifeboat alongside long enough for one of the two men to, firstly, throw a small dog across and then jump himself. The other man hesitated and,

54ft Arun *Edward Bridges (Civil Service & Post Office No.37)*, one of only three Aruns built with a wooden hull, served at Torbay from 1975 to 1994. FROM A POSTCARD IN THE AUTHOR'S COLLECTION

54ft Arun *Edward Bridges (Civil Service & Post Office No.37)* saved almost 300 lives during her career at Torbay, and she is now on display as part of the Lifeboat Collection at Chatham Dockyard. FROM A POSTCARD IN THE AUTHOR'S COLLECTION

52ft Arun *Marie Winstone* with 17m Severn *Alec and Christina Dykes* on the day the Severn first arrived at Torbay. NICHOLAS LEACH

The lifeboat house in Brixham harbour was built in 1873 but modified and altered many times, most recently for the D class inshore lifeboat. NICHOLAS LEACH

before he could jump, the lifeboat was carried clear. Further efforts to bring the lifeboat alongside proved fruitless as the lighter was driven further up the beach.

A line was then thrown to the man who pulled himself through the water. However, ten feet from the lifeboat he let go and was too weak to continue. Despite the motion of the lifeboat making it difficult, he was hauled aboard by the lifeboat crew, unconscious, and two lifeboatmen tried to revive him, but without success. For this service the Silver medal was awarded to Coxswain Thomas, the Bronze medal to Mechanic Richard Harris, and the thanks of the Institution on vellum accorded to the rest of the crew.

An inshore lifeboat station was established in May 1964 and an inflatable inshore lifeboat (ILB) was operated until 1970. A rigid-hulled ILB was then supplied for use both on inshore rescues and as a boarding boat. The stationing of such a craft at Torbay followed the evaluation

trials in July 1969 of the Hatch rigid-hulled ILB 18-03, a prototype design, which served in an operational capacity between 1970 and 1974. Another type of rigid-hulled ILB, the 18ft 6in McLachlan A-512, was sent to the station in March 1975 and served for twelve years.

In August 1975, a new lifeboat, the 54ft Arun *Edward Bridges (Civil Service & Post Office No.37)*, was sent to Torbay. She was a new design of lifeboat that was still being developed, and the boat sent to Torbay was only the third of the class to be built and the first that was 54ft in length. She stayed for nineteen years, launched 456 times on service and is credited with saving 285 lives.

The most outstanding rescue performed by *Edward Bridges* during her nineteen years of service took place on 6 December 1976 after the motor vessel *Lyrma*, of Panama, got into difficulties seven and a half miles south-east of Start

52ft Arun *Marie Winstone* on exercise off the harbour. NICHOLAS LEACH

The D class inshore lifeboat *John William Hirst* (D-651), which was placed on station in October 2005, in the boathouse. NICHOLAS LEACH

17m Severn *Alec and Christina Dykes* at moorings in the harbour. NICHOLAS LEACH

Point in a southerly storm and very high seas. The lifeboat put out at 1.15am and, after attempts to rescue the crew by helicopter were abandoned, had to be taken alongside to effect a rescue.

Acting Coxswain Keith Bower took the lifeboat in to the casualty's starboard quarter on numerous occasions during a difficult and daring undertaking. Four men were taken off during the lifeboat's first five approaches, but the lifeboat was damaged on the next attempt. Despite this the boat continued with the rescue, and two more survivors and the Master were taken off in three more runs. The last two survivors were picked up by liferaft. For this service the Gold medal was awarded to Acting Coxswain Bower, and Bronze medals went to the rest of the crew.

In January 1987 a standard ILB was sent to the station as the RNLI phased out the rigid-hulled ILBs, only a handful of which were built. A small portable building was used as a temporary house for the first inflatable ILB until, in 1989-90, the lifeboat house in the south-eastern corner of Brixham harbour, built originally in 1873, was completely refurbished and adapted to accommodate the ILB and also provide improved crew facilities.

Edward Bridges was taken out of service in 1994, and for the next seven years the station operated the former Fishguard Arun lifeboat *Marie Winstone*. After performing 280 service launches, this Arun was replaced in October 2001 by the 17m Severn class lifeboat *Alec and Christina Dykes*, which was funded from the bequest of the late Mrs Helen Christina Dykes, of Torbay.

17m Severn *Alec and Christina Dykes* has been on station at Torbay since 2001. BY COURTESY OF RNLI

The old lifeboat house, built in 1878, just above the Higher Ferry, some way from the sea; it is now occupied by Dartmouth Amateur Rowing Club. NICHOLAS LEACH

DARTMOUTH

A pulling lifeboat was operated from Dartmouth for less than twenty years during the last quarter of the nineteenth century. A lifeboat station was established following a public meting at which local people petitioned the RNLI to organise a new station. The Institution's management committee approved the station's establishment in July 1876 and a lifeboat was supplied in 1878. The boat, a 33ft self-righter, was named *Maud Hargreaves* in memory of the donor's daughter. She served for nine years but did not perform any services and was replaced in September 1887 by a new 34fft ten-oared water-ballasted self-righter.

This second, and last, pulling lifeboat, which was built by Forrestt at Limehouse, was named *Henry and Amanda Shaw* after the donor and her late husband. At her inaugural launch on 20 September 1887 it was stated that 'even in fine weather navigation is difficult for entering the port, and in a south-easterly gale there is a very great risk passing the narrow channel flanked by rocks'. She performed the station's one and only service launch, on 11 January 1894, to the trawling ketch *Princess of Wales*, of Brixham, which stranded near Kingswear Castle. Four lifeboatmen went aboard the casualty to help with the pumps, and the ketch was eventually beached safely.

The lifeboats were kept in a lifeboat house built at Sandquay at a cost of £480 during the summer, but taken to a mooring in Marfleet Creek during the winter so that they were more quickly available if needed. However, it is likely that, when an onshore wind caused casualties in Start Bay, getting the boat out of the harbour if it was needed was more or less impossible, although at the inaugural ceremony of the first lifeboat in October 1878 the hope was expressed that tugs would be available. The boathouse, which was used until the station closed in 1896, is still standing, sited just above the modern Higher Ferry,

Launch of relief D class inflatable *Bob Savage* (D-520). NICHOLAS LEACH

19

20TH CENTURY LIFEBOAT DEVELOPMENT

1904 A pulling lifeboat is fitted with a petrol engine to become the first powered lifeboat.

1909 The first purpose-built motor lifeboat completed.

1918 First motor lifeboats in Devon enter service at Torbay and Appledore.

1932 First lifeboat fitted with a diesel engine, which offers greater range and better fuel economy.

1963 The inflatable inshore rescue boat, later inshore lifeboat (ILB), is introduced; the first ILB in Devon is stationed at Torbay in 1965.

1967 The 44ft Waveney, based on a USGG design, introduced into service to become the RNLI's first design of fast lifeboat, and the tenth sent to Plymouth in 1974.

1975 First 52ft Arun sent to Devon and stationed at Torbay; the Arun was introduced by the RNLI in the early 1970s and became one of the most successful lifeboat designs ever.

1994 New 25-knot designs of lifeboat, the 17m Severn and 14m Trent, entered service, with Severns going to Torbay and Plymouth in 2001 and 2003 respectively.

Bob Savage (D-520) was the first ILB at the Dart lifeboat station after it was opened in 2007. NICHOLAS LEACH

some way from the sea; it has been used by the Dartmouth Amateur Rowing Club for many years.

In September 1896 the RNLI decided to close the station and the area around Start Bay, as well as the entrance to the Dart estuary, was covered by the large sailing lifeboats operated at the flanking stations of Salcombe and Brixham. For well over a century Dartmouth was without a lifeboat, until in 2007 moves to establish an inshore lifeboat came to fruition.

The D class inflatable ILB was sent to the station in October 2007 for evaluation and housed in a temporary building in Coronation Park under a five-year planning agreement pending the construction of permanent buildings; the new station was known as Dart lifeboat station and was formally established by the RNLI's Trustee Committee on 7 November. A couple of relief ILBs were supplied before the station's own new D class inflatable, D-702, was placed on station on 25 July 2008. Funded by Caterford Foods, she was named *Spirit of the Dart* and dedicated during a ceremony on 2 August 2008.

The naming of *Spirit of the Dart* (D-702) on 2 August 2008 by Mrs Barbara Felton. PAUL RICHARDS

The current Dart inshore lifeboat *Spirit of the Dart* afloat after her naming ceremony in August 2008. PAUL RICHARDS

The lifeboat house built at South Sands in 1869 for the station's first lifeboat and used until the station closed in 1925; the house is now used as a store, and remains largely unaltered.
NICHOLAS LEACH

SALCOMBE

Salcombe is well known as a holiday resort and sailing centre in an area of unspoilt natural beauty, surrounded by peaceful countryside. Its lifeboat station, which dates from the late 1860s, was established following the wreck of the ship *Gossamer*, of Liverpool, at Prawle Point on 10 December 1868 with the loss of thirteen crew. The following year the RNLI decided to open a station at Salcombe, and a 'very handsome' lifeboat house was built at South Sands on a site given by the Earl of Devon. This was used by the four pulling

and sailing lifeboats that were operated until the station was closed in 1925.

The most notable event in the era of the pulling lifeboats was the capsize on 27 October 1916 of the lifeboat *William and Emma*. She had launched to the assistance of the schooner *Western Lass*, which had gone ashore on the east side of Prawle Point in a severe gale. The crew of the vessel was rescued using rocket apparatus before the arrival of the lifeboat. As the lifeboat was heading home, she capsized just outside the bar at the entrance to the estuary and thirteen of her crew of fifteen were drowned.

Despite this terrible loss for Salcombe's small community, another lifeboat was supplied to the station in 1917. She was a 35ft self-righter named *Sarah Ann Holden* and proved to be the last pulling lifeboat. The station was closed in the mid-1920s as the motor lifeboats recently stationed at Torbay and Plymouth were deemed to provide adequate cover. However, this decision was reversed when it was evident that a station between these two was needed, and a 40ft motor self-righter, *Alfred and Clara Heath*, was placed in service in December 1930. Kept on moorings in the middle of the estuary, she was reached from the quay by boarding boat.

Alfred and Clara Heath served Salcombe for eight years until May 1938,

The Liverpool type lifeboat *William and Emma*, which served from 1904 to 1916, capsized on service on 27 October 1916 after launching to the schooner *Western Lass*. The crew of the vessel was rescued by the Coastguard before the arrival of the lifeboat, which capsized just outside the bar drowning thirteen of her fifteen crew.

The 35ft self-righter *Sarah Ann Holden* was the last pulling lifeboat to serve at Salcombe.

6,000-ton steamer *Louis Sheid*, which had picked up sixty-two survivors from another steamer, *Tajandoen*, which had been sunk by enemy action. *Louis Sheid* went aground in Bigbury Bay when she struck a rock off Thurlestone. Crossing the bar was difficult for the lifeboat because of the state of wind and tide, but once the lifeboat crew found the casualty, forty men jumped across to the lifeboat which then made for Hope Cove where the survivors were ferried ashore.

The lifeboat then returned to the steamer, but getting alongside this time was more difficult. However, once she was in position, a further twenty-two survivors were taken on board and then to Hope Cove. The lifeboat returned to the steamer for a third time, by when the vessel had been driven onto the cliffs and the rocket apparatus team had a line aboard. The remaining men were taken off by this, while the lifeboat stood by. For this rescue, the Silver medal was awarded to Coxswain Edwin Distin, who showed magnificent seamanship both in crossing the bar and alongside the steamer.

In June 1962 the first of three lifeboats to be funded by the Baltic Exchange came

when a 46ft Watson motor lifeboat, *Samuel and Marie Parkhouse*, was sent to the station. This boat, specially designed and built to cope with the dangerous bar at the mouth of the estuary, was known as the 'Salcombe' sub type and incorporated a lighter draught, whalebacks fore and aft to throw off the water, an after shelter carried forward to cover the engine room and a strong stern frame in case she should strike bar.

Samuel and Marie Parkhouse was involved in a number of fine rescues during the Second World War. On 7 December 1939 she launched to the

The first motor lifeboat at Salcombe was *Alfred and Clara Heath*, built in 1922 originally for service at Brixham.

The unique 46ft Watson 'Salcombe' type lifeboat *Samuel and Marie Whitehouse* served the station for almost twenty-five years.

Samuel and Marie Whitehouse was sold out of service in September 1963 after almost twenty-five years at Salcombe. This photo shows her at sea off Salcombe in 2005 when in private hands, for she remains largely unaltered externally although has been renamed *Oniros*. NICHOLAS LEACH

The 47ft Tyne *Baltic Exchange II* at moorings in the middle of the estuary. NICHOLAS LEACH

to Salcombe. The new boat was a 47ft Watson cabin motor type and spent twenty-six years on station during which she saved seventy-six lives. The most notable incident in which she was involved saw her become the second Salcombe lifeboat to capsize on service. She was turned over in severe weather on 10 April 1983 but fortunately no lives were lost as the air-bag deployed to bring the lifeboat upright.

The *Baltic Exchange* was on service to an upturned inflatable dinghy in a gale force nine, gusting to force eleven. As the lifeboat approached the casualty, she was hit by a huge wall of water which caused her to turn over. The air-bag, fitted so the boat would right in the event of a capsize, automatically inflated and the lifeboat successfully righted. All members of the crew were immersed during the capsize, and one was washed overboard, but he was quickly recovered once the boat was upright. The lifeboat was not damaged, and was able to proceed to Brixham after the casualty had been saved by a helicopter. Framed letter of appreciation signed by the Chairman, The Duke of Atholl, awarded to Coxswain Graham Griffiths and the crew in recognition of their determination following the capsize.

Launch of Atlantic 75 *Joan Bate* (B-794) at the end of her naming ceremony, 17 April 2003. PAUL RICHARDS

The ILB house for Atlantic 75 built in 2003 next to the crew building on the harbour front. NICHOLAS LEACH

16m Tamar *Baltic Exchange III* arrives on station in March 2008 escorted by 47ft Tyne *Baltic Exchange II*. NICHOLAS LEACH

The next Baltic Exchange-funded lifeboat, named *The Baltic Exchange II*, arrived in August 1988. The new boat was a 47ft Tyne, steel-hulled lifeboat capable of twice the speed of the boat she replaced, and was ideally suited for conditions at Salcombe. She saved 115 lives at Salcombe, with her most notable rescue coming on 8 January 1992. She launched in the early hours to the 1,200 ton coaster *Janet C*, which had suffered total power failure in south-westerly gale force winds and heavy sea.

On reaching the scene, the lifeboat crew made several attempts to transfer a line across to the coaster, and eventually a tow was connected. The coaster had been drifting towards the rocks, but once the tow was established the casualty was slowly pulled clear and then held for three hours until the arrival of a tug. For this service, the Bronze medal was awarded to Coxswain/Mechanic Frank Smith in recognition of his courage, seamanship, and determination during the rescue.

When the lifeboat was placed afloat in

16m Tamar *Baltic Exchange III* alongside the quay after she arrived on station with 47ft Tyne *Baltic Exchange II*. NICHOLAS LEACH

16m Tamar *Baltic Exchange III* on exercise off the Salcombe estuary. NICHOLAS LEACH

The station's Atlantic 75 inshore lifeboat *Joan Bate* (B-794) on exercise. NICHOLAS LEACH

the 1930s, operations were moved from South Sands to the town, and the renovated Unity Building on the harbour front was converted for use as a crew room. It was modernised in 1992 to provide good crew facilities, and on the ground floor has a museum and display area, a meeting room, toilet, shower and a reception area. In 2003 an Atlantic rigid-inflatable inshore lifeboat was sent to the station, and a new ILB house was constructed next to the crew building to house the boat. At the same time a new mooring pontoon berth for the all-weather lifeboat was provided near the Quay.

The facilities were built in readiness for the new 16m Tamar class lifeboat *Baltic Exchange III*, the third lifeboat to be funded by members of the Baltic Exchange in London, which arrived at Salcombe in March 2008. She was named and dedicated at a ceremony on 17 May 2008 by Mrs Gail Drayton, wife of the Chairman of the Baltic Exchange, at which a number of former lifeboats was in attendance, including *Oniros*, the station's former lifeboat *Samuel and Marie Parkhouse* which first arrived at the station exactly seventy years ago to the day and the Tyne lifeboat *Baltic Exchange II*.

16m Tamar *Baltic Exchange III* is the newest all-weather lifeboat in Devon. NICHOLAS LEACH

LIFEBOATS ON STATION: SOUTH DEVON

Exmouth
12m Mersey *Margaret Jean* (12-21), carriage launch, on station 7.5.2008
D class inflatable (D-669) *George Bearman*, trolley launch, on station 28.9.2006

Teignmouth
Atlantic 85 *The Two Annes* (B-809), tractor and carriage launch, on station 1.8.2006

Torbay
17m Severn *Alec and Christina Dykes* (17-28), afloat, on station 31.10.2001
D class inflatable *John William Hirst* (D-651), trolley launch, on station 10.2005

Salcombe
16m Tamar *The Baltic Exchange III* (16-09), afloat, on station 10.3.2008
Atlantic 75 *Joan Bate* (B-794), do-do trolley launch, on station 7.11.2003

Plymouth
17m Severn *Sybil Mullen Glover* (17-35), afloat, on station 15.2.2003
Atlantic 75 *Millennium Forester* (B-775), boathoist, on station 1.5.2004

Alec and Christina Dykes on exercise.
BY COURTESY OF RNLI

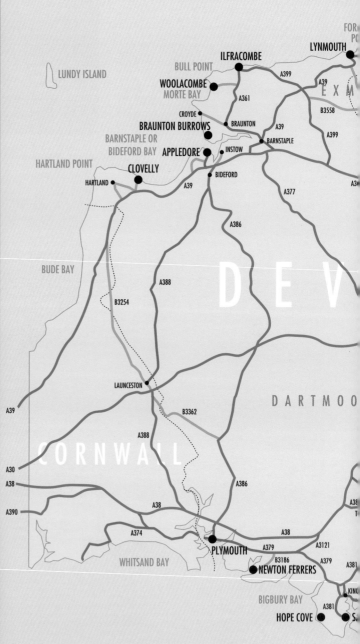

The Ilfracombe lifeboat *Spirit of Derbyshire* inside the lifeboat house, as seen from the viewing gallery installed for the benefit of visitors.
NICHOLAS LEACH

LIFEBOATS ON STATION: NORTH DEVON

Clovelly
Atlantic 75 *Spirit of Clovelly* (B-759), tractor and do-do carriage, on station 5.10.1999

Appledore
Tyne *George Gibson* (47-027), afloat, on station 19.6.1988
Atlantic 75 *Douglas Paley* (B-742), trolley launch, on station 11.12.1997

Ilfracombe
12m Mersey *Spirit of Derbyshire* (12-007), carriage launch, on station 20.7.1990
D class inflatable *Deborah Brown* (D-555), trolley launch, on station 1.8.2000

Map labels:
M5
A39
A39
B3223
A358
B3224
SOMERSET
A30
A358
N
M5
A373
ILMINSTER
A30
DORSET
HONITON
A358
A377
A30
A35
AXMINSTER
A375
A3052
A35
EXETER
A3052
A3052
LYME REGIS
A35
SEATON
A376 B3178
SIDMOUTH
LYME BAY
A38
A379
BUDLEIGH SALTERTON
A380
EXMOUTH
382
TEIGNMOUTH
N
BOT
A379
0   5 mile
A380 A3022
TORQUAY
0   5 km
85
PAIGNTON
TORBAY
BERRY HEAD
● LOCATION OF LIFEBOAT STATIONS
BRIXHAM
DARTMOUTH
TART BAY
ART POINT

HOPE COVE

Hope Cove is at the easternmost point of Bigbury Bay which, during the early nineteenth century was the scene of more than a dozen wrecks, but it was not until the 1870s that the lifeboat station was established. Following the wreck of the brigantine *Theodor*, of Hamburg, on 14 February 1874 when three men were lost after the vessel went ashore at Thurlestone, local residents applied to the RNLI for a lifeboat.

The lifeboat house built in 1877–8 is in use as a store, with the memorial stones to the donors set into the walls still intact. NICHOLAS LEACH

In March 1877 the new station was approved and a lifeboat house was completed in 1878 on a site given by the Earl of Devon. The first lifeboat, a standard 35ft ten-oared self-righter, arrived on 28 February 1878. Named *Alexandra* after HRH Princess of Wales, she was formally inaugurated at Kingsbridge on 13 June 1878 when she was drawn through the streets on her carriage.

Alexandra served Hope Cove for less than ten years, during which time she is credited with saving nineteen lives. She was replaced in November 1887 by a new lifeboat, also named *Alexandra* having been funded by the Freemasons. In fact, the four pulling lifeboats to serve Hope Cove were all so named, and all funded by the Freemasons. The second *Alexandra* was another standard self-righter, 34ft in length with ten oars.

After just over twelve years on station, the second *Alexandra* was found to be going rotten so was sold locally. Her replacement, which arrived in June 1900, was the former Newquay lifeboat *Willie Rogers* which had

The plaque commemorating the donors of the lifeboat and boathouse when the station was established in 1878.

been built in 1892 and was appropriated to the Freemasons. She stayed for only three years during which time she did not perform any services.

In July 1903 the fourth and final *Alexandra* lifeboat arrived. She was a non-self-righting Liverpool type, broader at 10ft in beam than the self-righters, less likely to capsize, and well suited to sailing. She had a twenty-seven year career at Hope Cove, saving two lives and launching eighteen times on service making her by far the busiest of the Cove's lifeboats.

No services were performed during the Second World War and, with only one service undertaken during the 1920s, in April 1930 the RNLI decided to close the station as the motor lifeboat at Salcombe cover the area adequately. The boathouse has remained standing and has been used as a store.

YEALM RIVER

The river Yealm, to the east of the busy port of Plymouth, was sometimes used as a refuge for ships but its narrow entrance restricted the size of vessels that could enter. A number of wrecks occurred in the vicinity during the nineteenth century, but the one which was the reason for the founding of the lifeboat station was the rescue of the steamship *Aivali*, of Marseilles. The steamer got into difficulties on 14 February 1874 and the local Coastguards saved the steamer's crew of nine.

Local residents asked for a lifeboat station to be established and in March 1877 the RNLI opened a station at the Yealm River, where plenty of fishermen were available to form a crew. A lifeboat house and slipway were built at the tip of the peninsula formed by the Yealm and Newton creek, on the outskirts of Newton Ferrers. The location was ideal for launching, but getting to sea involved having to cross the bar, which was often difficult.

The first lifeboat was a standard 35ft self-righter which arrived in March 1878. Funded by an anonymous gift, she was named *Bowman* when inaugurated on 27 April 1878. The first lifeboat performed only one service, assisting the Plymouth lifeboat on 28 January 1885 to save the barque *Wellington*, and was replaced in 1887 by another self-righter. The new boat, a 34ft craft built by Woolfe at Shadwell, was named *Darling* and was an improvement over her predecessor as she was fitted with water ballast tanks making her more suitable for sailing.

Darling performed five services, but saved no lives and was replaced in 1904 by what proved to be the station's last lifeboat. The new lifeboat, a 35ft self-righter named *Michael Smart*, arrived in April 1904 and was the most successful of the Yealm lifeboats, saving two lives and performing nine services.

The station, like that at Hope Cove, was closed during the 1920s when motor lifeboats came into operation. Although Yealm was considered suitable for a motor lifeboat, Plymouth was seen as better in terms ease of maintenance and refuelling so the lifeboat was withdrawn from Newton Ferrers in early 1927. The lifeboat was auctioned on 25 March 1927 and sold to a local owner for £72 10s to be converted into a pleasure boat.

The lifeboat house built in 1878 at Newton Ferrers is still standing, having been converted into a private residence after serving throughout the life of the Yealm River station. NICHOLAS LEACH

The 34ft pulling and sailing lifeboat *Escape*, which served at Plymouth from 1885 to 1898.

PLYMOUTH

Plymouth lifeboat station, one of the oldest in Devon, was established during the first decade of the nineteenth century. Its first lifeboat was funded by Philip Langmead, MP for the area, with a contribution from the Corporation of Lloyd's, which funded a number of other lifeboats around the country at the time including one for Exmouth, described above. This boat was, like the Exmouth one, a North Country type built by Henry Greathead to his design. Also like that at Exmouth, the boat was not liked by local boatmen and was never used.

The next lifeboat was provided in 1825 by the embryonic National Institution (RNIPLS), and operated from Cawsand at the mouth of the harbour. It was a 26ft non-self-righting type built by Plenty, of Newbury, who was responsible for designing and building the RNIPLS' first standard lifeboat. However, despite wrecks continuing to occur near Plymouth, the lifeboat, like its predecessor, was never used and was transferred to the Isles of Scilly in 1840.

The 37ft self-righter *Eliza Avins* aground in the aftermath of the Christmas Hurricane of 1912. She launched to the schooner *Ottawa* but, having saved five from the casualty, grounded. Left high and dry on the tide, she was subsequently got off and none of her crew was injured.

More than two decades passed before the next lifeboat came on station. The RNLI, following the reforms of the 1850s, included Plymouth in the expansion of lifeboat provision undertaken during the latter half of the nineteenth century. In

1861 a decision was made to establish a station and a 34ft self-righting lifeboat arrived in February 1862. To house the new boat, a lifeboat house was built on the western side of Millbay. This was used until 1898 when it was replaced by a new lifeboat house and launchway constructed at the Camber, near the West Pier, in Millbay Docks.

The new lifeboat was named *Prince Consort* and was involved in a very fine rescue on 8 December 1872, when in a south-westerly gale, she was towed out by an Admiralty steam tug to save four from the brigantine *Eliza* and eight from the brig *Fearful*. She was so badly damaged during this incident that shortly afterwards she was replaced by a new lifeboat.

Prince Consort was the first of three 34ft self-righters to serve the station between its reopening in 1862 and 1898, when the new boathouse was built to accommodate a larger boat. The others were named *Clemency* (1873-85) and *Escape* (1885-98) with the former having the honour of being present for the ceremony of laying the foundation stone of the new Eddystone lighthouse by HRH The Prince of Wales and the Duke of Edinburgh on 19 August 1879.

The new lifeboat sent to the station in 1898 was a 37ft ten-oared self-righter named *Eliza Avins*. She saved twenty-seven lives during her twenty-four year career at Plymouth, operating from the new boathouse at the Camber which enabled her to get out to sea more easily. In 1922, when she was found to be unfit for further service, she was replaced by another pulling self-righter, the 1904-built *Brothers Freeman*, but she was only as a temporary measure before a new motor lifeboat arrived.

The motor lifeboat sent to Plymouth was one of only four 60ft Barnett class boats to be built. They were twin-screw craft, the first lifeboats with twin engines to see RNLI service, and were the largest lifeboats ever built, weighing over forty tons. The Plymouth boat, the third of the class, was named *Robert and Marcella Beck* and arrived on station on 1 June 1926. Non-self-righting, she was powered by twin 76hp Weyburn DE6 engines which gave her a top speed of more than nine knots. The hull was divided into five watertight compartments and was fitted with more than 100 air cases.

The new motor lifeboat operated from moorings in Millbay Docks, as she was too large for any boathouse, and she remained on station until 1952 during which time she is credited with saving a total of seventy-two lives. Her most outstanding rescue took place on 13 January 1942 when she went to a Sunderland Flying Boat of the Australian Royal Air Force which had been carried on to the rocks in very rough seas. After several attempts, the lifeboatmen managed to get a line across to the casualty and then towed her to safety to save the two men on board. For this outstanding rescue the Bronze medal was awarded to Coxswain Walter

The impressive 60ft Barnett *Robert and Marcella Beck* was one of the first twin-screw motor lifeboats in the RNLI fleet.

Robert and Marcella Beck standing by the stranded steamer *Umberleigh* on 20 September 1930. She landed eighteen of the crew from the casualty.

Crowther and Thanks of the Institution on vellum to each of the eight lifeboat crew.

Unusually, *Robert and Marcella Beck*'s service at Plymouth was interrupted during the Second World War when she was requisitioned by the Admiralty in March 1943, and stationed in Iceland with the Fleet Salvage Officer for life-saving service on the hazardous northern convoy route to Russia. In July 1945 she was sent back to Scotland and also went to Blyth and Grimsby before returning to Plymouth in February 1946. She went for overhaul and did not return to her station until February 1947. While she was away her place was taken by a Belgian lifeboat, the *Minister Anseele*, which was picked up derelict in the English Channel early in the war, repaired and lent by the Belgian Government to the RNLI.

Robert and Marcella Beck was replaced in March 1952 by another Barnett, a 52ft type with twin 60hp diesels which gave her a top speed of just over eight knots.

Thomas Forehead and Mary Rowse leaving Millbay Docks on 16 February 1967 to assist the crabber *Silent Waters*. BY COURTESY OF THE RNLI

The 52ft Barnett *Thomas Forehead and Mary Rowse* was on station from 1952 to 1974.

Thomas Forehead and Mary Rowse with her successor, the 44ft Waveney *Thomas Forehead and Mary Rowse II.*

The new boat, named *Thomas Forehead and Mary Rowse,* was built by J. S. White at Cowes. During more than twenty years of service, she launched 169 times and became the busiest of the station's lifeboats hitherto, saving sixty-three lives.

Thomas Forehead and Mary Rowse was reaching the end of her operational life when she was involved in an outstanding service. On 16 January 1974 she went to the assistance of the Danish coaster *Merc Enterprise,* which was in difficulties twenty-six miles south of Rame Head in hurricane force winds and phenomenal seas. The lifeboat faced extremely heavy seas as she battled to the scene. When the coaster capsized, seven survivors were picked up by helicopter and as conditions were so bad the lifeboat was advised to return to station. However, with men still missing Coxswain John Dare carried on, but the lifeboat crew could see no sign of any survivors. For his courage, determination and excellent seamanship during this extremely taxing rescue, Coxswain Dare was awarded the Bronze medal.

Later in 1974, when the RNLI marked its 150th anniversary, the focus of the celebrations was on Plymouth where the first Lifeboat International Exhibition was held during July and August. Lifeboats from many countries were on display, including both old and new lifeboats from the RNLI. The opening ceremony was performed by HRH The Duke of Kent who arrived at the Royal Western Yacht Club on board the station's new lifeboat, *Thomas Forehead and Mary Rowse II.*

The new lifeboat was a steel-hulled 44ft Waveney class boat, powered by twin 260hp General motors diesel engines, and capable of speeds up to sixteen knots making her faster than any previous Plymouth lifeboat. She was placed on station on 22 May 1974, was christened on 17 June 1975 by HRH The Duchess of Kent, and served until September 1987. She gained an outstanding record of service, launching 181 times on service and saving ninety-one lives.

The most outstanding rescue by *Thomas Forehead and Mary Rowse II*

44ft Waveney *Thomas Forehead and Mary Rowse II* served the station from 1974 to 1987.

52ft Arun *City of Plymouth*, seen at moorings in Millbay Docks, served Plymouth from 1988 to 2002 during which time she saved 115 lives.

tookplace on 15 February 1978 when she was launched to the trawler *Elly Gerda*, which was in difficulties off Looe Island. By the time the lifeboat arrived the wind had reached gale force eight with conditions deteriorating. She stood by for several hours in the violent storm and very rough seas. The trawler eventually went aground on the Rennis Rocks so the lifeboat moved in. After two passes, two of the casualty's crew were saved.

As the lifeboat prepared to make a third approach, to save the skipper, the vessel was washed off the rocks. It then steamed eastwards under its own power, and was escorted by the lifeboat into Looe harbour. The lifeboat returned to

Plymouth just after midnight on 16 February, having been at sea for almost fourteen hours in dreadful conditions. For this rescue, Bronze medals were awarded to Acting Coxswain Patrick Marshall and Mechanic Cyril Alcock in recognition of their courage, determination and seamanship.

During the 1970s and 1980s, boarding arrangements were gradually improved. The Waveney was moored in Millbay Docks, as previous lifeboats had been, but in 1976 a new crew facility was built on the Princess Royal Pier and in 1979 mooring piles were provided which enabled the lifeboat to be kept moored alongside, thus improving boarding arrangements. In 1988, due to the redevelopment of Millbay Docks, the station was relocated to Sutton Harbour, where a berth was obtained in the Marina. However, in 1992 the station moved back to Millbay after a new berth was found in the newly-opened Marina. The three-storey octagonal Customs Office, originally built in the early nineteenth century and situated at the end of Millbay Pier, was restored and refurbished to become a crew building.

By the time the station had relocated to Sutton Harbour, a new lifeboat was in service, the 52ft Arun *City of Plymouth*. This

17m Severn *Sybil Mullen Glover* arrives on station on 11 February 2003 escorted by relief Arun *Newsbuoy*. NICHOLAS LEACH

34

The three-storey Customs Office, built in the early 19th century, situated at the end of Millbay Pier, was restored for use as a crew building in 1993. NICHOLAS LEACH

The Atlantic 75 *Millennium Forester* (B-775) in the hydrohoist berth in Millbay Marina. NICHOLAS LEACH

boat had been largely funded by the City of Plymouth Appeal under the patronage of the Lord Mayor of Plymouth, Councillor Tony Parish. The Arun was larger and more powerful than the Waveney it replaced, being fitted with two 485hp Caterpillar 3408TA diesels giving a speed of eighteen knots. Built at a cost of £592,478 by Souter Shipyard at Cowes, *City of Plymouth* was placed on station on 26 January 1988. She served the station for fourteen years and launched an incredible 579 times during that time, saving 115 lives.

As well as the offshore lifeboat, inshore lifeboats have also served at Plymouth and an inflatable ILB was sent to the station in May 1967, but was withdrawn in July 1968 and replaced by a rigid-hulled ILB. Between 1968 and December 1983 a series of these unusual ILBs were on station, and kept at moorings in the harbour close to the offshore lifeboat. Just over two decades later, on 31 March 2004, an Atlantic 75 rigid-inflatable, named *Millennium Forester*, was sent to the station. The boat was kept on a hydrohoist, which lifted the boat out of the water when not in

use ,and was moored in the Marina near the lifeboat moorings.

The station's present lifeboat is the 17m Severn *Sybil Mullen Glover*, which arrived in February 2003. The only Severn class in Devon, the lifeboat was named at a ceremony on 23 July 2003 by HM The Queen when she was in Plymouth to present a new Colour to the Royal Navy, and the station was marking its 200th anniversary. The Severn is the most powerful lifeboat to serve at Plymouth, and her twin 1,050hp Caterpillar engines give her a top speed of twenty-five knots.

Sybil Mullen Glover at moorings in Millbay Marina. NICHOLAS LEACH

35

The lifeboat house built in 1870 in the harbour and extensively altered in 1892.
BY COURTESY OF RNLI

The 35ft 6in motor self-righter *City of Nottingham* on trials; she was the first motor lifeboat to serve at Clovelly.
BY COURTESY OF RNLI

CLOVELLY

The small fishing village of Clovelly runs down a 400ft cliff and is one of the most picturesque coastal settlements around the British Isles. The Clovelly Estate was acquired by the Hamlyn family in 1738, and the family still owns the village. A lifeboat station was established here by the RNLI in 1870 after a number of wrecks had drawn attention to the hazards of the area. A lifeboat house was built on the harbour shore, and this house was rebuilt on the same site in 1892, with a stone slipway constructed on the foreshore to improve launching in the harbour.

The station's first lifeboat was a 33ft ten-oared self-righter named *Alexander and Matilda Boetefeur* which cost £320 and was built by the RNLI's boatbuilders Forrestt at Limehouse on the Thames. She was the first of three self-righting pulling

and sailing lifeboats that served the station well into the twentieth century. The other two, which served from 1893 to 1907 and from 1907 to 1936, were funded from the gift of Mr and Mrs John Roget and named *Elinor Roget*.

In the 1930s a motor lifeboat, the 35ft 6in motor self-righter *City of Nottingham*, was sent to the station. She arrived in June 1936, having been built in 1929 for the Hythe station in Kent, and served just over twelve years until being replaced in December 1948 by a 35ft 6in Liverpool motor type named *William Cantrell Ashley*. The first motor boat was single engined, but the new Liverpool class lifeboat was powered by twin 18hp Weyburn engines. She was re-engined in 1964 with twin 32hp Parsons Penguin diesels which gave her a greater radius of action.

The difficulties of launching at Clovelly are well illustrated by this photo of *William Cantrell Ashley* being dragged across the beach.

Arrival on station of 35ft 6in Liverpool motor *William Cantrell Ashley*, September 1949.

35ft 6in Liverpool motor *William Cantrell Ashley*, moored in the harbour at Clovelly, was on station from 1949 to 1968. *From an old postcard supplied by Graham Brailey*

William Cantrell Ashley was involved in a medal-winning rescue on 28 July 1954. She went to the motor ketch *Progress*, which had suffered engine failure near Lundy Island in very rough seas. Getting alongside the vessel was difficult as the lifeboat's approaches had to coincide with the rolling of the casualty. Ten runs were made over the course of an hour until the ketch's crew of three had been taken off, together with a variety of domestic animals, including a cat and its kittens. For this rescue, the Bronze medal was awarded to Coxswain George Lamey.

In 1968 *William Cantrell Ashley* was withdrawn and a 70ft Clyde cruising lifeboat, one of only three such lifeboats to be built, was placed on station and kept at moorings off the harbour. The intention was for her to be manned by a full-time crew and cruise the Bristol Channel, one of only two stations operating this cruising lifeboat, the other was Kirkwall. In reality, such a manning arrangement proved too costly and the boat was based for much of the time at Clovelly until needed on a

The prototype 70ft Clyde class lifeboat *Charles H. Barrett (Civil Service No.35)* at Clovelly; she was designed as a cruising lifeboat to cover the waters of the Bristol Channel.

The third 70ft Clyde lifeboat *City of Bristol* served at Clovelly from 1975 to 1988.

The original lifeboat house as rebuilt in 1999 to accommodate Atlantic 75 and launching tractor. NICHOLAS LEACH

Atlantic 75 *Spirit of Clovelly* (B-759) is launched at the end of her naming ceremony, 1 June 2000. PAUL RICHARDS

specific call. When this lifeboat was withdrawn in August 1988, following the station of a fast lifeboats at Padstow and Appledore, the RNLI closed the station.

However, the life-saving tradition off Clovelly was maintained between 1990 and 1997 by an 18ft rigid-inflatable named *Pride of Clovelly*. Operated, funded and managed by the Clovelly Trust, she was housed in the RNLI's lifeboat house. In 1997 the RNLI took over the station and again became responsible for its operation, training crew during the year in readiness for placing an Atlantic 21 on temporary station duty operating from the original lifeboat house. On 14 May 1988 the Atlantic 21 *Foresters* was declared

operational, and plans for a new lifeboat were made. This boat, the Atlantic 75 *Spirit of Clovelly*, was placed on station on 5 October 1999 and named at a special ceremony on 1 June 2000 by HRH The Duke of Kent KG, RNLI President.

To house the Atlantic and her launching rig, the lifeboat house, which has Grade II listed building status, was completely renovated internally in 1999. It was also extended so that the boat and launching tractor could be accommodated, while suitable crew facilities were also provided. A house was built to the east of the boathouse in 2005 for the bulldozer used to smooth out the rocky beach.

Launch of relief Atlantic 21 *Round Table* (B-543) on exercise; this lifeboat was on temporary duty from 1998 to 1999 shortly after the RNLI took over the station. NICHOLAS LEACH

APPLEDORE

Located around the treacherous Taw and Torridge bar and estuary, the lifeboat stations at Appledore, Northam and Braunton have a somewhat complicated history, particularly during the nineteenth century when lifeboats stationed at several different locations around the estuary.

The first lifeboat arrived in February 1825 and was an 18ft non-self-righting type named *Volunteer*, built by Plenty of Newbury. She was one of twelve boats built by Plenty for the nascent RNIPLS. The boat was managed by the Bideford District Association, one of several local organisations affiliated to the central body, and was housed in the King's Watch House overlooking the estuary. *Volunteer* was a small boat and weighed only one ton, but her sturdy construction stood her in good stead for she served the station for thirty years and is credited with saving at least eighty-eight lives.

In 1831 the station was taken over by the North Devon Humane Society, which had a substantial stone boathouse built at Watertown, half a mile closer to the Burrows than the Watch House. The new boathouse was large enough for two lifeboats, and in August 1831 the Society applied to the RNIPLS for another boat. A 26ft boat was built to the design of George Palmer and, named *Assistance*, she reached the station on 27 December 1831.

In the 1840s, following a wreck which *Volunteer* could not reach, the idea of stationing a lifeboat on the north side of the Taw/Torridge estuary was raised, together with providing a larger and more powerful lifeboat at the Watertown site. Following the wreck of the schooner *Albion* on the North Tail in December 1845, with the loss of six out of seven in the crew, the need for a lifeboat to the north of the estuary was more pressing than ever. So, in 1848 a station was established at Braunton Burrows, and *Assistance* was transferred there. The station was

The lifeboat was moved into the King's Watch House in 1829, where it was kept until 1831; this building is still in existence, albeit much altered, at the top of the slope leading down to the present station at Badsteps. NICHOLAS LEACH

THE MODERN LIFEBOAT FLEET

The RNLI currently operates five different types of all-weather lifeboat, all of which are in service at stations in Cornwall. In addition, Atlantic 75 rigid-inflatable and D class inflatable inshore lifeboats are in service.

Severn
17m x 5.5m,
speed 25 knots, afloat

Tamar
16m x 5.5m,
speed 25 knots, slipway or afloat

Trent
14m x 4.53m,
speed 25 knots, afloat

Tyne
47ft x 15ft,
speed 17 knots, slipway or afloat

Mersey
12m x 3.8m,
speed 16 knots, carriage

remotely sited amongst the sand dunes, and crews usually came from Appledore via a long overland trek and a ferry crossing.

A new lifeboat had been built for Appledore, named *Petrel*, and she arrived in October 1848. The boat, built by Thompson at Rotherhithe, does not appear to have been particularly successful initially for she was returned to her builder in January 1851 and rebuilt. Originally 28ft long, her size was increased to 30ft by 7ft and her oars to twelve from ten. However, she was no more successful after the alterations, and in 1851, with the North Devon Humane Society experiencing financial difficulties, when the station was taken over by the RNLI she was replaced.

The Institution decided to provide a new 30ft twelve-oared Peake self-righter and move operations to Northam Burrows, on the south side of the river entrance, where the boat would be nearer to help vessels on the South Tail, in the same way that the Braunton station covered the North Tail. A substantial new stone-built boathouse was built at Northam Burrows and the new lifeboat, which was named *Petrel* like her predecessor, was soon installed.

Volunteer remained at the Watertown station until 1856, by when she was beyond her serviceable life, and so was replaced by a light 'second class' Peake self-righter named *Mermaid*. *Mermaid* was also stationed on the Burrows in a house adjoining the old one, and at this point the Watertown station was closed. There were thus two lifeboats at Northam Burrows, and this was the case during two periods of the station's life, 1856 to 1861 and 1870 to 1889, so a numbering system was adopted, and the stations were known as Appledore No.1 and Appledore No.2.

Meanwhile, at Braunton Burrows, *Assistance* remained on station until 1857, by when funds were available to replace her with a small 28ft Peake self-righter named *Dolphin*, a sister to *Mermaid*. In 1862, for administrative reasons, a Barnstaple and Braunton branch was formed to manage the station, and for the next thirty-two years it was no longer part

of Appledore but was called Braunton station in its own right. However, the crew still came from Appledore.

In April 1866 one of the latest 32ft ten-oared self-righters was supplied, named *George and Catherine* after her donors Mr and Mrs Jeremy, of Axminster. *George and Catherine* served the station for fifteen years and saved twenty-one lives, before being replaced by the first of three lifeboats named *Robert and Catherine*, which were donated by Miss Leicester of Bayswater. A 34ft self-righter pulling ten oars, *Robert and Catherine* arrived in August 1881 and was the most successful of the Braunton lifeboats as she saved thirty-four lives during her twenty-one years on station.

She was replaced in July 1902 by a second *Robert and Catherine*, a 34ft Rubie self-righter, which was in turn replaced just ten years later after she capsized on 21 December 1911 while on exercise, fortunately with no loss of life. The new boat, a standard 34ft self-righter of the same name, arrived in May 1912, and served for just seven years. In 1918 the station had to be temporarily closed as almost all the launchers and the farm horses had been called up into the forces. However, with a motor lifeboat imminent at Appledore, the temporary closure became permanent in 1919.

The station on the sand dunes at Northam Burrows was operational between 1852 and January 1897, and was served by several small, standard self-righting lifeboats. The longest-serving of these was *Hope*, a 34ft standard self-righter, which was on station for almost thirty years, from 1862 to 1890, during which time she is credited with saving fifty-nine lives.

A new lifeboat station was established on the north side of the river at Braunton Burrows in 1848, and a boathouse was built to the north of the lighthouse at Airy Point; the crew were ferried across the estuary to the station. The station at Braunton Burrows was temporarily closed in 1918 as many of the launchers had been called to serve in the war; it was permanently closed the following year.

The first motor lifeboat at Appledore was the 40ft self-righter *V. C. S.*, which served from 1922 to 1938.

Because larger sailing lifeboats, and subsequently motor lifeboats, could be operated more easily from Appledore, where the crew lived, a station was reopened there in 1889. A lifeboat house was built at Badsteps with a stone slipway over the river foreshore enabling a launch directly into the river. The 34ft self-righter *Jane Hannah MacDonald*, which had been built in 1885 for the No.2 station, was transferred from Northam Burrows and this spelled the end for that station. Although *Hope* remained there until 1890, and two other lifeboats were sent for short periods, in January 1897 it was closed and operations were moved to Appledore.

The 1885-built *Jane Hannah MacDonald* was the first of three lifeboats so named, the last of which served from 1910 to 1922 and proved to be the last pulling lifeboat on station. By 1919 the RNLI was looking to provide a motor

lifeboat to Appledore, which was seen as a key station as it was centrally placed to cover Bideford Bay and beyond. In preparation for a new motor lifeboat, substantial alterations were made to the 1889-built boathouse and down the slipway rails were laid for a bogie carriage.

The new motor lifeboat arrived in May 1922. Named *V. C. S.*, she was a 40ft motor self-righter powered by a single 45hp four-cylinder petrol engine. The boat was named and dedicated on 18 August 1922 by Miss White, daughter of the Rev J. B. White, President of the Branch. *V. C. S.*, the first motor lifeboat in North Devon, served at Appledore from 1922 to August 1938 during which time she saved fourteen lives.

In 1938 a larger motor lifeboat was sent to the station, the 46ft Watson motor type *Violet Armstrong*, and she was kept afloat at moorings in the river off Badsteps,

The specially-modified 46ft Watson motor lifeboat *Violet Armstrong*, which served Appledore for twenty-four years and is credited with saving sixty-two lives.

and reached by boarding boat which was housed in and launched from the boathouse. *Violet Armstrong* was specially modified for working on the bar, having a lighter draught than the standard 46ft Watson, as well as a strengthened stern frame below the rudder post for protection should she strike the bottom. To help clear the seas more quickly she had turtle decks for and aft and a long streamlined shelter over the engine room.

Violet Armstrong gave good service throughout her career at Appledore, and she was replaced in May 1962 by another Watson motor lifeboat, 47ft in length, then the latest and largest version of the

Watson design. Named *Louisa Ann Hawker*, she served at Appledore for a quarter of a century and saved more than fifty lives. She was powered by twin 60hp Gardner diesels which gave a top speed of almost nine knots.

Louisa Ann Hawker was involved in an outstanding rescue soon after she arrived on station. On 17 November 1962 the Royal Fleet Auxiliary tanker *Green Ranger*, while under tow of the tug *Caswell*, parted her towline off Hartland Point in gale force winds and drifted ashore south of Hartland Point. *Louisa Ann Hawker* put out into the northerly gale, with conditions on the bar extremely bad.

The 47ft Watson motor *Louisa Ann Hawker* leaving the estuary.

47ft Tyne *George Gibson* has been on station at Appledore since 1988, and is due to be replaced by a Tamar class lifeboat in 2010. NICHOLAS LEACH

When *Green Ranger* was located, the tanker was lying on the rocks with her starboard side awash and seas breaking over her. Coxswain Cann manoeuvred his lifeboat alongside and instructions were called using the loud hailer, but there was no response from the tanker's crew, so Coxswain Cann got clear. The lifeboat stood by until 3.15am when a message was received that all survivors from *Green Ranger* had been landed by breeches buoy so the lifeboat returned to station. For this attempted service the silver medal was awarded to Coxswain Sidney Cann and the Thanks Inscribed on Vellum was accorded to the other members of the crew.

In 1972 an inshore lifeboat was sent to the station. The ILB, which was kept in the 1889 boathouse and launched down the slipway, was number B-500, one of the first of the Atlantic 21 rigid-inflatables to enter service. She was followed by another Atlantic 21 B-520 *Wildenrath Wizzer* which served for twelve years before being replaced by B-565 *Manchester and District XXXIII*. The Atlantics were ideal rescue craft for the conditions in and around the estuary and could cope admirably with the dangerous conditions often found on the bar. The current ILB is the Atlantic 75 B-742 *Douglas Paley*, which went on station in December 1997.

In June 1988 *George Gibson*, a 47ft Tyne class lifeboat, arrived on station. Funded by Mr George C. Gibson OBE, through the Gibson Charitable Trust, she was a steel-hulled self-righter powered by twin 425hp General Motors diesels giving her a top speed of about eighteen knots. Her naming ceremony was held on 25 June 1988 when by Mrs Frank Homfray, daughter of the donor, christened the boat.

George Gibson was involved in a fine rescue on 31 March 1994 when the fishing vessel *Torridge Warrior* suffered engine

47ft Tyne *George Gibson* at her moorings in the estuary, with Atlantic 75 *Douglas Paley* setting out on exercise. NICHOLAS LEACH

Atlantic 75 *Douglas Paley* is the latest rigid-inflatable lifeboat to serve at Appledore, and was placed on station in December 1997. NICHOLAS LEACH

failure off Bideford Bar Buoy in a strong gale and very steep seas. The lifeboat found the casualty making little headway on only one engine, so a line was passed across and it was towed clear of the bar. Because conditions on the bar were so severe, the only option was to go to Ilfracombe, and Ilfracombe lifeboat *Spirit of Derbyshire* launched to assist.

Atlantic 75 *Douglas Paley* is recovered outside the lifeboat house completed in 2001 on the site of the 1889-built boathouse. NICHOLAS LEACH

The wind had increased to force ten by this time, and, with a big following sea, towing the casualty proved very challenging. When the tow parted another tow line had to be rigged, the fishing boat was brought carefully round and Ilfracombe lifeboat took up the tow. By 4pm all three boats were off Ilfracombe, but had to wait for three hours for the tide by when it was possible to enter. Following this outstanding rescue, Coxswain Bowden was awarded the Bronze Medal for his fine seamanship and skill, and Coxswain Andrew Putt of Ilfracombe was accorded the Thanks of the Institution on Vellum.

In 2000-01 a new lifeboat house and slipway were constructed on the site of the 1889 house, which was demolished to make way for the new house. Although the 1889 house had been altered at various times, including in 1980, when a first floor crew room was built, and in 1989, it was not large enough and so the new house was built to provide better housing for the ILB and boarding boat, as well as improved crew facilities.

The lifeboat house built in 1871 seen when the station was operational. The wall was added in 1872 to try to keep the sand back, and the side room added in 1877 for the crew and omnibus drivers who had brought them from Ilfracombe.

The scene during the inauguration for the first Morte Bay lifeboat *Jack-a-Jack* on 17 March 1871. The lifeboat, on station 1871 to 1892, was renamed *Grace Woodbury* in 1872.

MORTE BAY

In 1871 the RNLI established a lifeboat station at Morte Bay and a lifeboat house was built at Woolacombe for the first lifeboat. The station was established because of the difficulty in pulling the Ilfracombe lifeboat round Morte Point in westerly or north-westerly gales. The new station was intended to cover this eventuality, and as the lifeboat was launched by carriage it could be taken not only to any part of Morte Bay, but also south to Croyde Bay.

As there were no men to form a crew at the new location, the lifeboat was manned by Ilfracombe crew. In the event of a launch, a horse and cart would take the men to Woolacombe, just over six miles away, if it was impossible for the Ilfracombe lifeboat to reach Morte Bay. A sufficient number of men were enrolled at Ilfracombe to provide a second crew for the Woolacombe-based boat, and a former Coxswain, George Williams, was appointed as caretaker of the new station.

The station was in existence for less than thirty years, and was served by two lifeboats. The first boat was a standard 33ft self-righter pulling ten oars, which was funded by the Society of Bristol masters in the African trade and named *Jack-a-Jack* after an African settlement with which her donors frequently traded. Unfortunately the donors got into financial difficulty, and so in 1872 the station was appropriated to the legacy of Robert Atton, and the lifeboat was named *Grace Woodbury*.

The lifeboat only performed two services as launching from the west-facing beach through surf, particularly during westerly gales, was often extremely difficult. The only successful services took place in March 1883 when *Grace Woodbury* assisted the steamer *Lynx*, which had been run aground on Woolacombe Sands. The lifeboat landed the seven-man crew during the evening of 6 March, and the following day helped to successfully refloated the vessel.

In 1888 *Grace Woodbury* was taken to London for various improvements, but four years later she was condemned and sold. She was replaced by a larger 36ft self-righter, one of three lifeboats built from the legacy of the Rev T. S. Echalaz. However, *Theophilus Sidney Echalaz* performed no services while at Morte Bay

As the new century approached, it was realised that the station was probably not needed and in May 1900 the RNLI decided to discontinue it. The lifeboat was removed and subsequently transferred to Watchet. The boathouse, built in 1871 at the south-west corner of the village, still stands, and has been used as the Boat House Café for a number of years, albeit with several additions and external alterations.

The lifeboat house as it is today, much altered but still just about recognisable as a lifeboat house. NICHOLAS LEACH

ILFRACOMBE

The first rescue boat at Ilfracombe was a local pilot boat fitted out as a lifeboat, which was funded with the help of the RNIPLS in 1828 and cost £13 12s to fit out. No details of whether this boat was ever used or where it was kept exist. No further attempts were made to provide a lifeboat at Ilfracombe for more than twenty years and then, in 1850, a lifeboat was built by the Cowes-based builders Thomas and John White for the station.

The White-built lifeboat was a 32ft non-self-righting craft pulling twelve oars, and had been funded by local subscriptions and managed by a local committee known as the Ilfracombe Lifeboat Association. This organisation had Lloyd's Agent William Huxtable as its first honorary secretary, and a first lifeboat house was built at the corner of Hiern's Lane at the back of the harbour, with a slipway down into harbour. The boat is said to have been named *Lady Franklin* after the wife of the explorer Sir John Franklin. What became of this boat is unclear, although she is said to have decayed probably as a result of poor maintenance.

But by the mid-1860s approaches were being made to the RNLI by various influential local people to form a lifeboat station and the Institution established a station in 1866 and a new 32ft self-righting lifeboat was supplied, with a launching carriage. The boat was funded from the gift of Robert Broadwater, of London, and was named *Broadwater*. She

The boathouse built in 1893 beneath Lantern Hill was altered several times for larger lifeboats. In 1990 the house was extended and adapted to accommodate the Mersey lifeboat and it was replaced in 1996.

served until 1886 and is credited with saving forty-five lives during her two decades on station.

A lifeboat house was constructed for the new lifeboat near the foot of Lantern Hill, in the grounds of the pier, from where lifeboat could be launched directly into the sea down a slipway at Warphouse Point. However, in 1871 the slipway was filled in during the building of new wooden piers and, to launch, the lifeboat had to be taken through the town and round to the harbour, and down the slipway there to get to sea. In 1893 a larger lifeboat house was constructed under Lantern Hill on the site of the previous house.

In June 1886 the first of two lifeboats named *Co-operator No.2*, funded by the Co-operative Wholesale Society, was placed on station. She was a standard 34ft self-righter pulling ten oars and launched ten times on service during her six years on station. She was replaced in December 1893 by a new, larger self-righter, 37ft by 9ft, and pulling twelve oars, after it had been decided that a larger boat would be more suitable. This boat was given the same name as her predecessor and remained on station for almost thirty years, saving thirty-nine lives during that time.

The 37ft self-righter *Richard Crawley* being pulled through Ilfracombe's streets to the slipway into the harbour. She was the last pulling and sailing lifeboat at the station and spent fifteen years in service.

46

The Surf lifeboat *Rosabella* was the first motor lifeboat at Ilfracombe and served from 1936 to 1945.

The 35ft 6in Liverpool motor lifeboat *Robert and Phemia Brown* on her carriage outside the lifeboat house by Lantern Hill.
BY COURTESY OF GRAHAME FARR

The next Ilfracombe lifeboat, *Richard Crawley*, arrived towards the end of 1921. She had been built in 1910 for the Southsea station, near Portsmouth, and served there for eight years until the station was closed. She then became available and so was transferred to Ilfracombe. Like the boat she replaced, she was a standard 37ft self-righter but with various design improvements.

Richard Crawley was the last pulling lifeboat at the station and she was replaced in March 1936 by a new motor lifeboat. This boat, named *Rosabella* after the wife of donor John Hogg of Boscombe, was a light Surf lifeboat intended for carriage launching and working close inshore. She was the first of only nine Surf lifeboats to be constructed and was fitted with twin screws and twin 12hp Weyburn petrol engines. She had a speed of just over seven knots and carried fuel for ninety miles at her cruising speed.

The long-serving 37ft Oakley *Lloyds II* arriving on station in July 1966. She served for twenty-four years and saved 116 lives during that time.
BY COURTESY OF GRAHAME FARR

Rosabella served Ilfracombe for less than ten years, but was on station throughout the Second World War. She undertook eighteen wartime launches, seven of which resulted in services. Many of the launches proved to be fruitless searches for ships and aircraft believed to be in distress, and were often prolonged affairs carried out in terrible weather. When she was replaced at the end of the war, *Rosabella* was sold to the Netherlands lifeboat service which had a shortage of lifeboats following the wartime occupation by the Nazis.

The new lifeboat was a larger and more powerful Liverpool type boat, 35ft 6in in length, and fitted with a single 35hp Weyburn petrol engine. Named *Richard Silver Oliver*, she had served at Cullercoats and Newquay before coming to Ilfracombe, where she stayed for seven years and saved twenty-three lives during that time. The outstanding rescue in which she was involved took place on 13

12m Mersey *Spirit of Derbyshire* at speed off the pier for Lifeboat Day 1994. NICHOLAS LEACH

12m Mersey *Spirit of Derbyshire* emerges from her boathouse ready to be launched. NICHOLAS LEACH

Spirit of Derbyshire is readied for launching into the harbour at high water. NICHOLAS LEACH

November 1949 after the Spanish steamer *Monte Gurugu* lost its rudder in hurricane force winds and extremely violent seas, and was sinking south of Lundy Island.

Richard Silver Oliver encountered heavy breaking seas as she left harbour, but she battled her way through despite being filled with water on numerous occasions. After more than an hour at sea, the ship's lifeboat was spotted off Morte Point, with twenty-three of the crew on board. The lifeboat was able to pull the boat clear of the breakers and out to sea. The survivors, who were totally exhausted, were then taken on board the lifeboat and landed at Ilfracombe. For this rescue, the Silver medal was awarded to Ilfracombe Coxswain Cecil Irwin.

In October 1952 a new lifeboat, *Robert and Phemia Brown*, arrived on station. She was a 35ft 6in Liverpool type boat, similar to her predecessor but fitted with twin 20hp FKRS Kadency diesel engines which gave her a slightly greater speed and greater range. She was funded from the legacy of the late Captain Robert Brown, of Anstruther, and was formally christened on 20 August 1953 by a relative of the donor. *Robert and Phemia Brown* served at Ilfracombe for fourteen years undertaking essentially routine services until being replaced in July 1966 by a 37ft Oakley class lifeboat, *Lloyds II*. The Oakley, built at a cost of £34,000, was the most advanced lifeboat at the station hitherto as it was self-righting, thanks to an ingenious water ballast system, and was fitted with twin 52hp Parsons Porbeagle diesel engines. She served for twenty-four years, saving 116 lives in that time, and being involved in some very fine rescues.

The most outstanding rescue performed by *Lloyds II* took place on 9 September 1984 after the yacht *Liberty* got into difficulty, dragging its anchor in north-westerly winds gusting to gale force eight and very rough seas. The lifeboat reached the yacht just seven minutes after launching and found her only fifty yards from the shore. Despite the difficult conditions, a tow line was passed across from the lifeboat to the casualty, which was pulled clear. After cutting the yacht's anchor cable, it was eventually brought into harbour. In recognition of his courage, leadership and seamanship during this rescue, the Bronze medal was awarded to Coxswain David Clemence.

On 22 June 1990 a new 12m Mersey class lifeboat, *Spirit of Derbyshire*, arrived at the station. The new lifeboat, powered by twin 260hp Caterpillar 3208T diesels, had a top speed of seventeen knots, more than twice that of the boat she replaced and was a significant departure from all previous designs of lifeboat which had served at Ilfracombe. Aluminium-hulled, she had cost £444,498 to build and was funded by a special appeal in Derbyshire together with a local appeal organised by the Ilfracombe station.

In 1995-96 a new lifeboat house was constructed in the harbour, near the launching slipway, for the Mersey and D class lifeboats and launching tractor. The position of the new house meant that the lifeboat no longer had to be towed through the streets to be launched, and this speeded up the response time considerably. The new house included a workshop, souvenir sales outlet, crewroom, changing rooms, shower and toilet, and provided the modern facilities needed by the volunteer crew.

LYNMOUTH

The towns of Lynmouth and Lynton straddle the confluence of the West Lyn and East Lyn rivers, and are today tourist spots on the picturesque Exmoor coast. Although shipwrecks were not very frequent on this part of the coast, when the ship *Home* was wrecked in August 1868 this prompted calls for the establishment of a lifeboat station.

The lifeboat station was established in 1869 by the RNLI. the first lifeboat was a small 30ft self-righter, funded at a cost of £400 by a Yorkshire lady in memory of her brother, and named *Henry*. This boat arrived at Lynmouth on 20 January 1869 and was drawn by eleven horses on her carriage along the hilly road to her new station. Initially the lifeboat was kept in a shed on the Beach until a boathouse was built on the side of the little harbour on a site granted by the Lord of the Manor. It was rebuilt in 1898, and again in 1906-7 to accommodate a larger lifeboat.

Henry remained on station until April 1887 during which time she saved six lives. She was replaced by a larger 34ft self-righter, named *Louisa*, which was funded from the gift of the Rev Thomas Wheeler, of Worcester. This lifeboat, which saved twenty-four lives during her twenty-year career at Lynmouth, was involved in the most famous incident in the history of the station, which occurred in 1899 and has become one of the most famous rescues in the history of the RNLI.

At 7.52pm on 12 January 1899 the 1,900-ton three-masted ship *Forrest Hall*, carrying thirteen crew and five apprentices, got into difficulty off Porlock Wier in a severe gale. She had been under tow, but the tow rope had broken and the ship was now dragging its anchor. *Louisa* had to be launched to assist but, due to the terrible weather, it was realised that to launch at Lynmouth and row round to Porlock Wier would be impossible. Coxswain Jack Crocombe therefore proposed to take the boat by road to Porlock's harbour thirteen miles down the coast and launch from there.

The boat on her carriage weighed about ten tons, and just getting the whole rig up the one-in-four Countisbury Hill out of Lynmouth was a tremendous feat accomplished by twenty horses and 100 men. A number of men were sent ahead with picks and shovels to widen the road which, at its highest point, is 1,423ft above sea level. But the lifeboat reached the top, after more than ten miles of wild Exmoor tracks had been crossed. The descent of Porlock Hill was equally dangerous, with horses and men pulling

The last pulling lifeboat at Lynmouth, *Pritchard Frederick Gainer*, is hauled down to the sea on her carriage.

Pritchard Frederick Gainer on exercise during the late 1930s.

the ropes to prevent the carriage from running out of control.

The lifeboat eventually reached Porlock Weir at 6.30am and was launched to *Forrest Hall*. Although cold, wet, hungry and exhausted, the crew rowed for over an hour in heavy seas to reach the stricken vessel and managed to save the eighteen men on board, who had survived being stranded throughout the night. Amazingly there were no injuries amongst the rescuers or rescued, although four horses died of exhaustion.

Louisa was replaced in August 1906 by a new 35ft self-righter, *Pritchard Frederick Gainer*, which was the largest lifeboat to serve at Lynmouth, and had all the latest advances in design, including water-ballast tanks. She served for almost forty years, undertaking a number of good services during the First World War, and in total saved forty-one lives.

The station was closed at the end of 1944 as it was deemed to be no longer necessary, and the RNLI was planning for the

withdrawal of all pulling lifeboats. The lifeboat, *Pritchard Frederick Gainer*, was sold out of service in August 1944 and converted into the cabin cruiser *Lynmouth*. The old boathouse was used as a club until most of it was washed away during the disastrous floods of 15 August 1952. The boathouse was subsequently rebuilt and contains a small public shelter and display area in which can be seen a service board recording the rescues undertaken by the Lynmouth lifeboats.

The public shelter which was built on the site of the lifeboat house on the west side of the harbour.

A replica of the service boards from the Lynmouth station listing the rescues performed by the station's lifeboats.

50